AF323482

Isabella's Aviary
by Kristen Zajac

Photography by Trisha DeLaurent

Dedicated to my lovely young friend, Isabella, who has worked so hard to make an amazing dream come true; to her beautiful brilliant mama, Trisha, and her wonderful brothers, Max and Alex. Also dedicated to Small Blessings Preschool and their two special parakeets, my own beloved "Elfy" bird, and the social media sensation Disco, the fast talking budgie, all of whom led me to meeting Isabella in the first place.

Isabella's Aviary
Copyright © 2016 Kristen Zajac
Illustrations Copyright © 2016 Trisha DeLaurent
Hardcover ISBN: 9781616338206 1616338202
Paperback ISBN: 9781616338213 1616338210
eBook ISBN: 9781616338220 1616338229
December 2016
Published in the United States of America

GUARDIAN ANGEL PUBLISHING, INC.
12430 Tesson Ferry Road #186
Saint Louis, Missouri 63128 USA
http://www.GuardianAngelPublishing.com

Prologue

Isabella's eyes glistened as she watched over 20 species of exotic birds soar over Asia's Caravan stage at Disney's Animal Kingdom. Only ten years old, she could name them all; Blue and Gold Macaws, a Trumpeter Hornbill, Amazon Grey Parrots, Rose-breasted Cockatoos, a Great Horned Owl, a Harris Hawk, a Red Legged Seriema, and East African Crowned Cranes. She squeezed my hand with excitement as each new bird was introduced and took flight across the mystical set designed to look like an ancient Indian aviary from times past when Maharajahs ruled the land of India. As Disney's magnificent "Flights of Wonder" show progressed, I found myself equally torn between watching the majestic birds of every color, or the mesmerizing smile and joy of their most loyal and lovely admirer. Like the gorgeous winged creatures of whom she is so fond, Isabella filled the air with grace, color, life, and beauty. It is a joy and privilege to tell her story.

Early Years

Isabella's passion for birds and nature were inspired at a young age. She was born in January 2003 in Phoenix, Arizona. She and her family moved to Portland, Oregon when she was eight months old. This beautiful baby girl was a fighter and although as time went by, she had to spend many months in and out of the hospital, health issues never dimmed her radiant smile and spirit. Isabella embraced her family's move to Seattle, Washington when she was 8 years old. She spent adventurous days there enjoying the coastal seaport city's terrain and wildlife with her brothers. Despite ongoing medical problems, Isabella found joy in many things; Seattle lights, heron sightings in her backyard, waterfront lunches, and planting orchids with her mom.

At age 11 Isabella and her family returned to Portland, Oregon where she was happy to be reunited with her very best friend, Marcella. Her brothers, Max and Alex, led their sister on many adventures from pumpkin patches, trick or treating, and spirited Easter egg hunts, to games and practical jokes.

Most of all, they enjoyed the outdoors together, hiking and exploring.

A Girl With a Passion

Isabella's mom always loved birds, so Isabella was raised in a household with pet parrots, including a smart and mischievous Ruby Macaw, named Bentley, and two Eclectus birds named Mackie and Phineas. Isabella delighted in feathered friends right from the start as did her youngest brother, Alex, whom she affectionately referred to as 'my Baby Buggy'.

Since Bentley, Mackie, and Phineas were technically Mama's birds, Belle and Alex were overjoyed when she granted them the request to have pet birds of their own, two parakeets whom the children named Benny and Oliver. Isabella and Alex took their jobs seriously. Each day they helped their mom prepare food for their flock and enjoyed the birds' crazy antics. Together, they prepared seed and nut mixes for their little parakeets and a mix of organic grains, vegetables, fresh fruit, and legumes—a variety of beans—for their big parrots.

Mackie would stop by for a cuddle with Isabella and make her laugh as he tried to steal all the food from the other birds' bowls. When Isabella was sick, Mackie was there for snuggles. Isabella was sick a lot.

Dark Days

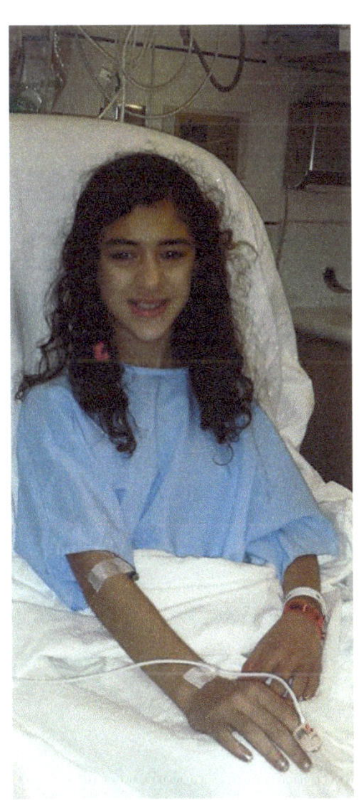

While most kids went home after school, Isabella often went to doctor appointments for a seizure disorder and other health issues. When she was 8, Isabella's health problems became much more serious. Isabella had a lot of stomach pain and problems. She lost a lot of weight. Since her stomach wasn't allowing her to eat all the good foods she needed to grow and feel good, she had to have a feeding tube inserted into her body and kept there to help her get all the right nutrients. Isabella's doctors searched for answers to the puzzle of what was going wrong with her health. Isabella bravely went to many more medical appointments and underwent more tests.

In January 2013, Isabella and her mom traveled to Pennsylvania to meet with a brilliant specialist.

During this stressful time of waiting to see what was wrong with her health, family friends Nick DiPaulo and Alicia Antheunisse met Isabella and her mom in Pittsburgh and cheered them up with a surprise visit to the National Aviary to see the birds.

After all the tests the doctors were able to make a diagnosis, the answer to the puzzle. She had a name for what was making Isabella so sick. It was a scary sounding word, "neurodegenerative disease".

It meant that Isabella's nervous system—the network of nerves and cells that carry messages to and from the brain and spinal cord to various parts of a person's body—was experiencing some problems. It meant that over time, parts of Isabella's body gradually might stop working as well as they should because the messenger nerve cells were having some trouble taking their orders from her brain to her body parts to make them do their jobs well.

Isabella was very brave. She did not let this diagnosis get her down, but her family and friends felt like their hearts had been torn into pieces because they loved her so much and wished her life could be easier for her. Although there were many supportive treatments and therapies to help with symptoms, problems, and pain from the disease, scientists were still searching for a cure.

Isabella's family grieved for the uncertainty of the future. It was hard to talk. It was hard to think. It was a dark time. They thought about experiences that seemed far away—things like watching Isabella graduate from college, get married, become a mother. And then in the midst of that darkness, that very brave girl with the beautiful brown eyes and curly raven hair looked up at them as if she could almost read their thoughts.

Full of excitement Isabella said one morning soon after, "Mommy, can my parakeets have babies so I can be a mommy, too?"

Her mama smiled, hugged her daughter, and said, "Yes!" Thinking back on that moment, she said it was a turning point as she realized in that one simple innocent request, a new future and purpose had opened up for them all and pushed the darkness away.

Dreams Take Wing

From that moment on Isabella and her mama, Trisha, became an unstoppable team. They reached out to their friend, Alycia Antheunisse, who owns Cedar Hill Birds, and asked which type of birds would breed quickly. Auntie Esha, as Belle calls her, and husband Eric surprised Isabella with the donation of a pair of Green Cheek Conures and a pair of cockatiels to support Isabella's dream. Mama and daughter drove to the airport to pick up the birds, laughing for joy, and talked animatedly about what they would name the two pairs.

"We should name the conures Tiki and Hula, Mama!" Belle grinned. "And let's call the cockatiels Jasper and Pearl. I can't believe they're mine!"

Belle was so excited to greet them at the airport, but she was also nervous that they would be very tired from the long flight since they had flown all day to see Belle. She and her mama decided they would make sure the birds got plenty of rest when they arrived at home.

Isabella couldn't wait until her birds had babies. On the ride home from the airport, Isabella talked a lot about how Bentley, Mackie, and her parakeets had given her comfort and friendship during difficult times. Suddenly, Isabella dreamed a new dream. She wanted other kids with health issues to be able to experience that same strength and love she had from companion birds. Isabella decided that some of her chicks should go to other special needs families. She set out to make her dream come true.

Belle and her mama arrived home from the airport with excitement and a renewed sense of purpose over Belle's new birds. Alicia and Eric's gift had planted the seeds of something very special.

While remembering those days, Isabella's mama Trisha said, "I had not seen my little girl light up with pure joy and excitement in such a long time. She was glowing inside and out since getting her babies."

"Belle was happier, more engaged, and even seemed to have more energy. Alicia and Eric didn't just give us two sets of birds, they gave us a much deeper lesson—that dreams, passion, and love heal the spirit even when medicine fails the body."

Isabella's Babies

Isabella's cockatiel pair, Pearl and Jasper, loved to be out of their cage and spend time with Belle, especially on her bed. Isabella enjoyed watching her new birds play and bird talk to each other and to her and preen/clean their feathers. As if to please their mother Isabella, Pearl and Jasper were also quick to take to their nest box and make her dream come true. They soon produced four eggs! Isabella excitedly brainstormed baby bird names with her mama and brothers. Soon the first baby chick hatched, a teeny tiny baby girl whom Belle named Harlow.

Harlow had quite a birth story as Belle's mama explained; "Harlow came into this world dramatic and screaming! Pearl and Jasper were first time parents and moved away from her screaming instead of caring for her. Because of this she became 'our' baby from day one. Isabella was mesmerized by her tiny size, and I was so intimidated!

"While I have hand-fed birds many times, I had never cared for something so defenseless from day one. I set Harlow up next to Belle's bed and always allowed Belle to hold her close and warm near feeding times. I got to watch my two little drama queens thrive!

"I got to watch them fall in love. I got to see Isabella's eyes light up to hold her baby and to watch Harlow snuggle close with absolute comfort. I got to watch Harlow choose Isabella, and Isabella choose Harlow. These girls were exactly what one another needed, and they were meant to be together!"

When Isabella described Harlow, it melted your heart. "Harlow is my best friend. She kisses me and loves me and keeps me safe." Isabella nicknamed Harlow—Harlow Who in honor of one of her favorite children's books, "Horton Hears A Who" by Dr. Seuss.

Even the family's Eclectus bird Mackie was fond of Harlow. "Mackie learned to say her name." explained Trisha, "Mackie kept hopping down to check on her and talk to her. He said 'Hi Baby. Good Harlow.' Harlow was in a tank so he could see her but couldn't get in with her, although he wanted to. You would have thought that Harlow was his own long lost baby, he was so mesmerized by her!"

While Pearl and Jasper were overwhelmed and unprepared for their first arrival, their maternal and paternal instincts kicked in as the next eggs hatched. While Trisha and Belle hand fed and hand raised baby Harlow, parents Pearl and Jasper were able to skillfully care for the next chicks. After Harlow's birth, the second chick to hatch was Raja, followed by Petrie, and finally Hope. Belle enjoyed singing to the babies and watching them grow.

Launching Isabella's Aviary

Belle and her mama cared for their growing flock and worked to make her dream of raising chicks for young special needs friends a reality. After a lot of planning and hard work, they launched Isabella's Aviary Alliance, LLC, dedicated to hand-raising and training baby cockatiels for special needs families.

As president, Trisha researched and recruited a team of ten esteemed board members to develop and implement long and short-range plans for the organization and oversee its charitable goals. (See Appendix One: Board Members.) They set up an official website and Facebook page for Isabella's Aviary and received immediate support from the public.

"We were shocked and humbled to see hundreds, and eventually thousands, of people not only join us, but offer their friendship, support, and love," said Isabella's mother Trisha. "Soon we had an amazing community dedicated to making my daughter's dreams come true."

What happened next would touch Isabella's heart and soul forever. The moment they heard her story and learned of her efforts, the American Federation of Aviculture (AFA) offered Isabella a membership and stepped up to be an official sponsor of Isabella's Aviary. Belle was overjoyed beyond belief and excited about the opportunities to participate in AFA conferences.

Unfortunately, she became ill and was unable to attend. Thankfully her Auntie Esha was able to step in, attend the conference, and accept on Isabella's behalf the essay award she had won. Isabella was disappointed to miss out on the opportunity of meeting sponsors and business community experts, but she knew there would be other opportunities in the future.

With the endorsement of the AFA, more and more generous sponsors within the bird community were thrilled with the idea of Isabella's Aviary. Belle's heart soared as additional business sponsors took up her cause, and her dream took flight.

Her mom said, "Kaytee/SuperPet generously agreed to sponsor both our aviary and adoptive families by giving cages and accessories like perches, dishes, and toys. Avian Biotech donated DNA sexing for all of our future chicks as they are born so we know which ones are boys and which ones are girls—with birds it is hard to tell otherwise."

Isabella and Trisha were moved by the support and sponsorship of countless individuals and businesses that donated resources and supplies to Isabella's Aviary.

"Barbara Heidenreich of Good Bird Inc. provided educational books and DVDs. AvianPRO agreed to exclusively sponsor our aviary and adoptive families with their quality food and treats. Additionally, many small private parrot toy manufacturers donated toys."

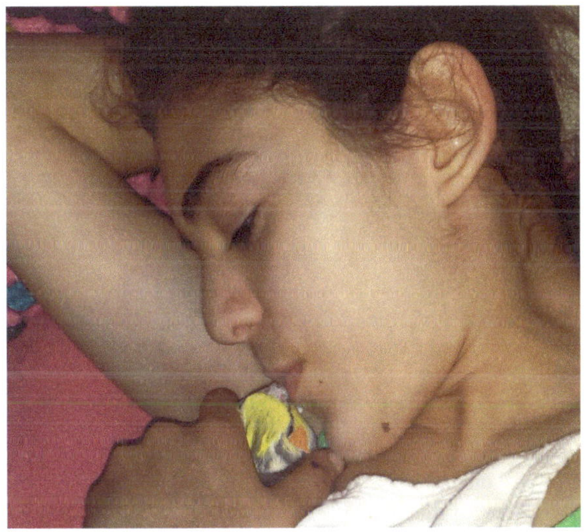

Two Hearts Come Together: Adoptions Begin

With a board of directors, a team of companies who were business sponsors, and a clutch of cockatiel chicks hand-raised and trained by Isabella, Isabella's Aviary was ready to make its first official placements. First up for adoption was Harlow, the baby chick who was rejected by her bird parents and exclusively hand-raised and fed by Isabella.

The decision by the Board of Directors was unanimous; the first official placement of Isabella's Aviary gave Harlow to Isabella. Those two belonged together!

Isabella was overjoyed; "Harlow is my best friend. She just likes to make me happy and be close to me. Sometimes she makes me laugh, other times she just wants to snuggle. I think all kids need a best friend, especially special kids because we are at home more and can't meet many other kids and do as many things."

Her mother said, "The two of them set the standard on which our Foundation could be based and carry forward into the future. We believe that with proper support and education, two hearts can come together and connect in a way that changes the lives of both for the better."

More Hearts Are Joined

Isabella and Harlow were the first of many perfect matches made possible by Isabella's Aviary. In August 2013, Isabella's Aviary and the Exotic Animal Foundation hosted a special event to celebrate their next parrot adoption, giving Primrose the cockatiel to a wonderful little girl named Brooklyn. The party was hosted at the home of Eric and Alycia Antheunisse at their Cedar Hills Bird Farm. Everyone who had supported Isabella's dream of starting an aviary was invited. The invitation read;

*"Isabella got sick and dreamed
of helping other special kids.
Brooklyn's brother has autism,
and she's his biggest helper.
Both girls love to help others
and share a passion for parrots.
Isabella raises companion birds.
Brooklyn is adopting the first one.
Friends and family celebrate
'A Place Where Dreams Fly';
An event to honor our pledge
to children and service outreach.
We thank you for attending
and supporting our dreams."*

It was an event that everyone who attended would always remember. Isabella had a lovely time at the party and was excited to help Brooklyn become a "Companionship Bird Parent" by giving Primrose to her.

Terese of the Central California Bird Club exclaimed about the adoption event at Cedar Hills Bird Farm. "It was a like a tropical dream. Big birds are everywhere…living on the patio, in the house, around the yard. It was magical. Kids were running everywhere, playing with birds and tortoises and dogs. What a blast! Watching this adoption happen was indeed magical. "

Five-year-old Brooklyn did not know what was happening until Isabella came out with a little cockatiel named Primrose and gave her to Brooklyn. She took the bird and clutched it to her and nuzzled its little face. At first she didn't understand, and then she said "She's mine?" There was not a dry eye in the house watching the bond between the two little girls and a little girl cockatiel."

Many other adoptions followed. Isabella's Aviary "Companionship Bird Parents", Edward (age 10) and Synthia (age 7) are both brave superhero kids who are role models to others as they deal with autism, asthma, and allergies. Also, Synthia did not let her epilepsy get her down, and Edward has bravely dealt with hypoglycemia.

Isabella's Aviary Board unanimously agreed Edward and Synthia were perfect companion birds parents given their keen interest in animals, their history, and knowledge of how to take great care of them;

Said Trisha DeLaurent, "These kids LOVE animals and even have cool bird murals on their walls! They currently have bunnies, a dog, and even a parakeet!"

Both children were excited to learn that they were selected to receive companion birds from Isabella's Aviary.

The Parrot Princess

As Isabella's Aviary continued to thrive and more birds were placed in adoptive families, word of her good deeds spread far and near. Isabella started getting messages of support from kids and parents all over the United States and even around the world. Isabella loved it when fans wrote to her and when some even donated money or supplies to her aviary, so more kids could receive a companion bird. Once in a while a fan even surprised her with something special for herself. One of Isabella's favorite surprises was when Edison's Art Clothing, a famous fashion designer in Hollywood California, learned of her aviary and designed and created a one-of-a-kind custom "Parrot Princess" dress for Isabella.

As a design feature of the dress, Edison's Art Clothing incorporated real feathers that Isabella's fans had contributed when their pet parrots molted (naturally shed feathers). The result was a gorgeous bright colorful gown, embodying both the beauty of the macaws and the lovely girl who so admires them. Isabella proudly wore her parrot princess dress to a special dance party at Walt Disney World during her Make-A-Wish trip in the fall of 2013. Radiant and absolutely stunning, Isabella captured all eyes and hearts as she swept across the dance floor in her beautiful gown. Everyone wanted to meet the enchanting and exquisite parrot princess who looked as magical as Cinderella at the ball. It was another dream that came true for Isabella.

While at Disney, Isabella also enjoyed many amazing surprises and behind the scenes experiences with feathered friends at the renowned Animal Kingdom. Nick DiPaolo, Vice President of Isabella's Aviary, had reached out to animal trainer and behaviorist, Barbara Heidenreich, a respected leader in the avian community. Barbara Heidenreich, in turn, called her contacts at Disney World, and they arranged a personal parrot experience for Belle at Disney's Animal Kingdom. It was a week Belle would never forget.

Isabella and her family had first row seats at the magnificent Flights of Wonder outdoor show. Belle could name all the birds, and her face glowed, watching them soar high into the sky above the crowd. After the show Isabella and her family were treated to an exciting backstage tour with the trainers where Belle got to meet all the birds and was even serenaded by some of the feathered friends who seemed to know the Parrot Princess was in their midst. Later she toured the Animal Kingdom's tropical aviaries. Birds of all colors and sizes flocked to see the Parrot Princess and greeted her with a chorus of song. They lived happily at the parts of the kingdom called the Maharajah Jungle and Pangani Forest. It was an experience and a trip Isabella will always remember and treasure. Isabella and her family are grateful to Make A Wish Foundation and Give Kids the World for making another special dream come true.

Heroes Come in All Shapes and Sizes

Since returning home from her trip, Isabella has continued to work hard at school and in her aviary, hand raising countless baby birds as companions for special needs children. It is something she believes in passionately and loves to do.

Isabella is fierce, brave, and determined. She doesn't let her illness stand in the way of her dream. Her persistence in overcoming the daily challenges of living with neurodegenerative disease has inspired many other kids and adults who are facing difficult times from an illness or health problem. Isabella has drawn upon her own experiences to do something good to help others, in fact, something quite magnificent.

When you ask kids what makes Isabella and her aviary so special, they consistently recognize Isabella as a leader who makes a difference in other children's lives.

Said Elizabeth Tucker (age 11), "Isabella took a leap of faith when she set out to start her aviary. Many adults would have totally given up when faced with the huge task of raising and training therapy birds but not Isabella. Thanks to Isabella, so many sick kids' lives have changed forever from having the companionship of these special birds. Isabella is a hero!"

Indeed, with grace and determination, Isabella has made a big dream take flight. Her work is a testament to the fact that you are never too young to make a difference.

By fostering a unique animal-human partnership, Isabella's Aviary is leaving a lasting legacy in families across the United States and changing lives one child and one bird at a time. Each bird placed matters to a special child, and each precious child matters to that treasured bird. It is a perfect match; a bond that empowers both child and feathered friend.

Isabella's Aviary is an intersection where faith, determination, and hope unite; a place where dreams fly and touch the sky. All those who have met Isabella as well as those who have been the recipient of one of her birds are forever changed.

On behalf of all those who have experienced her magic, we say, "Thank you from the bottom of our hearts, Isabella. We are inspired by you! We believe in your leap of faith and your acts of grace, lovely girl whose dream took flight. Your dream soars on in the flight of each bird, and your dream shines brightly in the smile of each child."

Epilogue

As I wrote this book, I had the joy and honor of spending a day at Disney World and Animal Kingdom with Isabella and her family. It was a day I will always treasure; sharing laughs, exchanging bird talk, and walking hand in hand with Isabella. In addition to her heart of gold, strong will, sense of humor, passion for birds and environmental conservation, I was greatly impressed and surprised by her fearlessness.

One little known fact about Isabella is that she LOVES roller coasters, the faster and wilder the better! During her Make-A-Wish trip at Disney, Isabella must have sought out and conquered every single scary roller coaster she and her brothers and Mom could find. Due to a neck injury sustained in a car accident, I was unable to join them for the roller coasters, but I took a chance on a log flume ride after Belle convinced me to accompany her on it toward the end of our day at the Magic Kingdom.

Before boarding Splash Mountain, I told Isabella she was very brave and that I wasn't nearly that brave.

Isabella turned to me with a serious and kind expression, took my hand in hers and said, "Miss Kristen, I believe you are indeed very brave."

As the log flume ride cascaded down waterfalls, Isabella jubilantly waved both hands high in the air, screaming with joy, while I protectively held one arm around her and the other on the safety bar. We both laughed together as we reached the final splash.

"Now *that* was a risk worth taking," she beamed. "How fun. I wish we could do it again!"

As I watched her for the rest of that fleeting day, her arms intertwined with those of her beloved mother and alternately embracing and teasing her brothers, I gained a true appreciation for that inner strength and spunk that makes her so special. Isabella, the dreamer, the risk taker, the one who keeps going no matter what stands in her way. As we talked about her aviary and the children to whom she had given companion birds, her face beamed with pride. She also gave me great tips on care of my own parakeet, Elfy!

In those treasured 10 hours we spent together, I knew I was in the presence of greatness; someone who gives more honesty, heart, and soul to the world. In spite of her medical circumstances, Isabella has accomplished more in her young life than many people do in their lifetimes.

Take a risk, make a change, leave a legacy; that is the spirit and intensity of Isabella's passion and zest for life, and the root of her 'can do' attitude in the face of adversity.

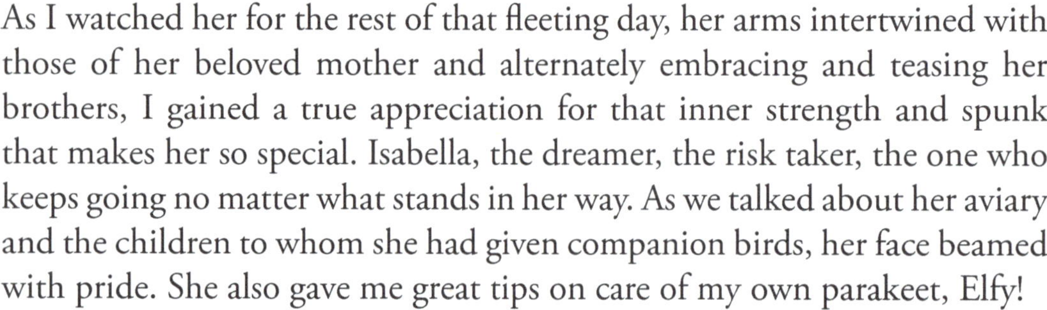

Trisha DeLaurent eloquently describes her daughter's demeanor; "Over the years I have watched my Isabella grow into such a strong, intense, and passionate little girl. Isabella is all, or she is nothing—halfway doesn't exist in her world. She is full of force but even fuller of heart.

"Some days she is gentle, sweet, and my emotionally fragile angel. Other days she is a firecracker that shapes the world to her will. Throughout it all she is authentic in a way that most people never are. Her thoughts and feelings always shine true, and because of that I have learned a lot about what it means to live life honestly."

Myself, I know that I am forever changed from meeting Isabella and seeing what she has accomplished in her young life. I am proud to call Isabella and her mother, Trisha, my friends. I hope you, too, will be moved by Isabella's story and inspired by her aviary, and maybe you'll even consider supporting it.

I hope it will go further than that though, that each of you will consider taking a risk yourself; to follow your own inner calling and take a chance, make a change, and do the one thing you know deep in your heart you were always meant to do. Do it for yourself, do it for Isabella, do it because the world needs each person's light to shine.

Appendix I:
-To learn more about birds and proper bird care, "like" and follow the public Facebook group Isabella and her mom started called **"Avian Answers- a Safe Place to Ask Questions and Get Answers"** at
https://www.facebook.com/groups/749518065063250/
-To stay up to date on Isabella's latest efforts and adventures, "like" and follow Isabella's Aviary on Facebook at
https://www.facebook.com/IsabellasAviary/ Stay tuned to these sites for updates and current information.

Please keep in mind that in addition to running Isabella's Aviary, Isabella and her mom and brothers are also a very busy family with many responsibilities. Isabella's Aviary will always be an active and involved participant in the parrot and special needs communities. However, there will be some periods of time where Isabella's Aviary will take a temporary hiatus from breeding and placing companion birds as Isabella and her family's school, health, and work commitments necessitate. You can check out Isabella's website for updates on her Aviary, all her feathered friends, and the family's latest activities.

Isabella, her mom, and brothers believe that following their hearts for advocacy has and will continue to lead to special avenues and opportunities to make a difference. One of Isabella's favorite quotes is "She believed she could, so she did." Isabella hopes that her Aviary and feathered friends will always have a special place in your heart.

Isabella also hopes you will make friends with and support kids in your own local community who are dealing with health issues or other challenges. Isabella says, "Be brave and follow your own dream to make a difference, wherever it leads you. Do not give up!"

Special Thanks

Isabella would like to take this opportunity to thank everyone personally who has helped make her Aviary dream a reality, including her wonderful Board of Directors and Corporate Sponsors. You mean the world to her and have allowed her to bless so many deserving kids with companion birds. Heartfelt thanks and appreciation.

Isabella's Aviary Board of Directors

Trisha DeLaurent, President
Nicholas DiPaolo, Vice President
Jason Crean, Director of Community Outreach and Educational Liaison
Bob Pfeifer, Director of Strategic Planning and Communications
Alycia Antheunisse, Director of Aviculture
Elva Kells, Director of Childhood Education and Enrichment
Rick Rowland, Director of IT Services and Website Management
Cynthia Cummins, Managing Member of Volunteer Coordination and Outreach Planning
Elizabeth Smith, Managing Member of Graphic Design
Mimi Estep, Managing Member of Family Support Services
Rollie Berrie, Managing Member of Social Hospitality

Corporate Sponsors of Isabella's Aviary

Kaytee
Avian Biotech International
The American Federation of Aviculture
IDA Cards
Good Bird Inc.
Parrot Safari Toy Factory
King Crayon
AvianPRO

An Interview with Harlow the Cockatiel (or "Harlow Who" as Isabella calls her.)
By Bentley the Macaw Diva

Bentley: Hello girls and boys! This is Bentley the Macaw reporting live from Isabella's Aviary. Today, I'd like to introduce you to Harlow the cockatiel. Harlow is going to teach us some more about cockatiels and how to take care of them. Harlow and I get the best bird care ever from our super cool mom, Isabella. Harlow, can you tell me who your favorite person is?

Harlow: Isabella, that's who!

Bentley: Why is Isabella so special?

Harlow: She is my mommy! I love her very much. She spends a lot of time with me. I have a big cage but I also get tons of time out of my cage every day. I love time to exercise and snuggle with my mommy. She also makes me delicious treats to eat! Yippee!

Bentley: How big should a cockatiel cage be, Harlow?

Harlow: Even though we cockatiels are small birds, we still need big cages so we have plenty of room to exercise. We can live up to 20 years and sometimes even up to 30. The first cage you buy us will probably be our home for life so please, please make sure it is big enough! We should have enough space to spread both wings out at the same time without touching either side of the cage. We also need a cage that is large enough to hold multiple perches so we can fly from one perch to the next. We also need enough room in the cage for toys, food and water dishes, and a cuttlebone.

Bentley: Humans usually like measurements, Harlow. Can you give me some numbers?

Harlow: Yes, Bentley! According to The Cockatiel Handbook by Mary Gorman, a cockatiel cage for a single bird should be no smaller than 20 x 20 inches (50 cm x 50 cm), but larger is better, I mean waaaaay better.

You need to increase the size of the cage by 30-50% for each additional cockatiel so everyone has enough space. Also, for safety, we cockatiels need cages with bars that are no more than a half inch apart so we don't get our bodies caught between the bars.

Bentley: Should you get a new cage or a second hand cage?

Harlow: Good question, Bentley! I usually prefer new cages. You must be careful with second hand cages and research them well. Sometimes older cages and cages imported from other countries can have toxic metal bars and you also have to make sure the previous bird who lived there wasn't sick with a contagious disease.

Bentley: Thanks for the guidance Harlow. We definitely want to make sure all our cockatiel friends have safe, large cages so they can live long happy lives and get lots of exercise. Let me ask you this. Once owners have purchased the large cage, what should go inside? How should they set it up to make their cockatiels happy?

Harlow: Another good question, Bentley. I am so glad you asked. Isabella knows how smart I am, so she always puts lots of perches, swings, toys, and treats in my cage for me. She also plays me music every day, all different styles of music. Isabella and I even have a favorite song, "Must Be the One," by She Wants Revenge. Woohoo! I just love my mom!

Bentley: Oh yes, my mom Isabella is great. Come here, Isabella! It's Bentley Boo! Want some kisses? Woohoo! You're a pretty girl! Ooh, such a good a goooood girl!

Harlow: Bentley, Bentley! Focus!

Bentley: OK, OK, now where were we?

Harlow: That I wish all bird owners could have a mommy as wonderful as Isabella. But she is all MINE so I will just have to share with everybody all she does so they can try to do the same. Isabella is awesome at bird enrichment. Enrichment is everything in the bird world. It is so important to keep your bird stimulated so he or she does not get bored or depressed. I highly recommend the book, Boredom Busters for Birds: Fun and Feather Friendly Toys and Activities, by Nikki Moustaki. It gives lots of great ideas about fun things like foraging pods, foraging toys, puzzle toys, swings, climbing structures, and homemade treats like birdy kabobs and fruit baskets. Yum! As bird expoert Nikki explains, "Enrichment can turn the average perch potato into an acrobat, climbing and swinging about his enclosure; a scholar, figuring out knotty puzzles; and an archaeologist, digging for buried treasure." Woohoo!

Of course, it is also important to consult your avian veterinarian and bird groups experts like the Facebook group Isabella and her mom Trisha launched, "Avian Answers-A Safe Place to Ask Questions and Get Answers" https://www.facebook.com/groups/749518065063250/ to ensure you put safe toys and objects in your bird's cage. Surprisingly, not everything sold in pet stores is safe. Birds can sometimes get caught in things that are not well made.

Bentley: Where should you go to buy a pet bird?

Harlow: Funny you should ask 'cause my mommy has very strong opinions on that!
Bentley: Do tell, Harlow!
Harlow: Isabella knows how smart we birds are, and it makes her sad that some people buy birds on impulse without doing the research to take good care of their feathered friends. Mom says a lot of birds are neglected or abandoned because people don't know how to care for us properly. They don't realize we need so much daily attention and mental stimulation, that we get emotionally attached to our special person, and that we have such a long life span.

If you are interested in adding a bird to your family, Isabella highly recommends seeking out a bird rescue group and rehoming a middle aged or older bird in need rather than buying a young bird from a pet store.

When considering rescue birds from an animal shelter or rescue organization, Isabella says "Don't let other peoples' impression of a bird influence your perception of that bird's capacity for love."

Isabella's loyal pet Morgan, an Amazon she rescued from a neglectful past, is a great example. Nicknamed "the Green Meanie" by others due to her formerly nasty temperament, Isabella has tamed Morgan and has become the love and center of Morgan's life. Morgan is as gentle with Isabella as she is with Morgan. Isabella believes that mean formerly abused birds make the best pets because once you earn their trust, they are loyal forever. She strongly encourages bird enthusiasts to consider adopting a bird with a rough history who deserves a second chance at a loving home. Isabella says you have to be willing to be patient and invest your time and heart.

Bentley: Well said, Harlow. Woohoo! Spread your wings, Girl! Here's to second chances, and here's to our amazing girl, Isabella! (Did you know she even got me my own pet chameleon in an aquarium to watch? Talk about bird entertainment!) To all our readers out there, this is Bentley Boo, signing off! We hope you enjoyed my interview with Harlow about preparing to add a feathered friend to your home. For more detail on diet and nutrition, grooming and maintenance, and medical care, please research online and visit your local library to learn about the specific needs of the bird you are adopting. Isabella's "Avian Answers-A Safe Place to Ask Questions and Get Answers" Facebook page is also a great place to seek advice.

Thank you for your time. Over and out!

CPSIA information can be obtained
at www.ICGtesting.com
Printed in the USA
LVHW072146150720
660696LV00004BA/18